NORFOLK CHILDREN'S HEALTHY COOKBOOK

Compiled and designed by

The Aquila Club
Kinsale Junior School
Hellesdon
Norwich
Norfolk

All the profits from the sales of these books will go to the
East Anglian Air Ambulance

Copyright

All material appearing in 'Norfolk Children's Healthy Cookbook' is believed to be copyright of its respective authors. No part of the material may be copied without first contacting the Headteacher of Kinsale Junior School.

If you believe that a recipe is your copyright and has been used without permission or incorrectly, then please contact the Headteacher of Kinsale Junior School.

We are hugely grateful to <u>Norse</u>, our main sponsor, without their support quite simply we would not have been able to turn our idea into the Cookbook you are holding now.

**PRINTED BY
2MPRINT
Unit 8, Longs Business Centre
232 Fakenham Road
Taverham
Norwich
NR8 6QW**

Contents

FOREWORD

INTRODUCTION

THE EAST ANGLIAN AIR AMBULANCE

HEALTHY EATING AND HEALTHY COOKING

THE RECIPES

- LIGHT MEALS AND SNACKS
- BREADS
- SOUPS
- SALADS
- BISCUITS AND CAKES
- DESSERTS
- DRINKS

GLOSSARY AND ABBREVIATIONS

TOP TIPS AND ESSENTIAL KITCHEN EQUIPMENT

OUR THANKS

Foreword

What a wonderful initiative this is - that the children of Kinsale Junior School are actually thinking about producing healthy recipes. Being born and raised in Norfolk and having gone to a local primary school I have learnt and am fully aware of what wonderful produce is available on our doorstep throughout the seasons and its lovely to think that the children of Kinsale Junior School at such a young age are learning about what is produced locally and at what time of the year different foods are in season.

Galton Blackiston

It's a great honour to preface the Norfolk Children's Healthy Cookbook, dedicating it to our highly skilled aircrew and all the illustrious doctors and paramedics, who have saved, and continue to save people's lives.

These delicious recipes have been carefully selected for their broad appeal; as I turned the pages it became increasingly obvious that it had become time to eat, and only a good cookbook makes this kind of impression.

Huge thanks to all those people with tremendous culinary talent who have whisked up these great recipes. I am sure most will take a little longer than the Air Ambulance's twelve minutes it has for maximum delivery time of a casualty to the nearest Accident & Emergency facility, but nonetheless; "Good things come to those who wait!"

Every copy of this book sold helps to keep those life-saving rotors spinning. The Air Ambulance relies almost exclusively on private charity to keep to its invaluable mission.

May you enjoy these fantastic recipes, designed to keep the wolf well away from the door and thanking you for helping such a great charitable cause.

Lord Iveagh
Elveden, Norfolk

INTRODUCTION

We are the Aquila Club from Kinsale Junior School in Hellesdon, Norwich. We are a small group of children that meet once a week before school and we like a challenge. At the beginning of the school year we gathered our ideas together and decided that our challenge would be to create a 'Norfolk Children's Healthy Cookbook'.

In previous years we have made a children's leaflet about Norwich City Centre and this leaflet was distributed from the Tourist Information Centre in The Forum, Norwich. We have also made a board game called 'Norfolk's Fine Food' which was a great success and is now sold nationwide.

We have gathered two types of recipes from both well known Norfolk adults and Norfolk school children. The children's recipes have been chosen by holding a competition for children aged between 5 and 11.

We wanted our recipes to be healthy as we would like to encourage people to have a healthy lifestyle and also to eat balanced diet.

We think that it is important to use locally grown ingredients or to even grow your own at home or at school. Using food from Norfolk reduces air miles and is better for our environment.

Every year we chose a charity to collect money for; this year we have chosen East Anglian Air Ambulance (EAAA). All profits from the book will be going to them. Hopefully lots of money will be heading their way!

At the end of each adult recipe we have quotes (*in Lucinda calligraphy*) that were written by children of Kinsale Junior who tasted them after the recipes were kindly cooked up by the Norse catering team.

We had great fun making this book and learnt so much. Thank you for buying our cookbook. We hope you like it, use it, enjoy cooking up the recipes and eating them.

Joella, Ailsa, Hashim, Louis, Callum, Bethany, Fraser, Riley, Lucy and Sophie.

THE EAST ANGLIAN AIR AMBULANCE

The East Anglian Air Ambulance provides a lifesaving service to the people of Norfolk, Suffolk, Cambridgeshire and Bedfordshire 365 days per year. We have two medically equipped helicopters and a team of highly skilled clinicians, who attend an average of 4 - 5 missions per day. The majority of these missions are road traffic related and many others being agricultural or equestrian. We do not receive any Government funding or National Lottery funding, so rely on the people of our region to raise over £4.2 million per year. We are delighted to have the support of Kinsale Junior School with their unique cookery book, and have been proud to assist the wonderful children at this school. We pass on huge thanks to all involved with this splendid book. We need you today. You may need us tomorrow.

Jess Down
Area Fundraising Manager
Norwich & North Norfolk
East Anglian Air Ambulance
Unit 5B Alkmaar Way, Norwich International Business Park, Norwich, NR6 6BF
Tel: 01603 489408

The Photographs
The first is an image of our (old) BK117 'Anglia One' helicopter, the second of our new red Bond aircraft and third was taken by professional photographer Julian Claxton.

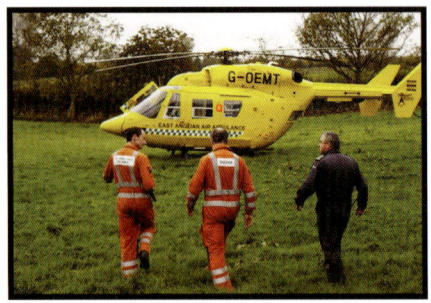

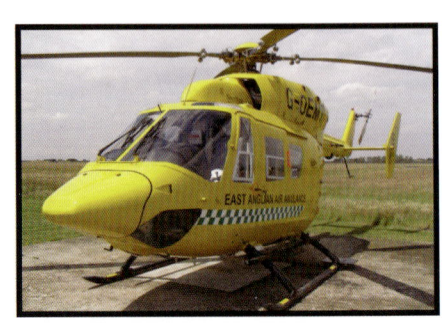

HEALTHY EATING AND HEALTHY COOKING

We know that you don't want us to write pages and pages about healthy eating, so we won't, however, as this is a 'healthy' cookbook we felt it should have a little bit about healthy eating which is very important for having a healthy lifestyle. This page is to explain to you how to eat a **balanced diet***, although, you may have foods that you do or don't like you must ensure that you eat the right things!

***Diet** means the food and drink usually eaten or drunk by a person or group.

'Going or being on a diet' means something else; 'when someone eats less food, or only particular types of food, because they want to become thinner or for medical reasons', don't get muddled up!

For more information visit www.nhs.uk/Change4Life

Our bodies are like amazing cars, you need the right type of fuel to keep running properly. If we do not have the right fuel we will not be as active and won't have as much energy.

Rice, bread and pasta (Carbohydrates)
These are the foods that give us our energy, about a third of our daily diet should come from this food group.

Meat, fish and eggs (Protein)
This type of food helps our body to grow and repair itself. These foods are vital to our body and we need to eat them every day.

Fruit and vegetables
Vitamins, minerals and fibre come from these foods which help us stay healthy; a third of our food should come from this group.

Milk, yoghurt and cheese (Dairy)
These dairy foods give us protein and also calcium to help us to have strong bones and teeth.

Sugar and fats
Too much of these can be bad for us so we only need a small amount.

We understand that everyone has their favourite foods; nevertheless, you need a variety of all the different food groups to live a long active life! It's all about getting the right balance!

Don't forget your **five a day**! (5 pieces of fruit and vegetables).

LIGHT MEALS AND SNACKS

THAI CURRIED COCONUT CHICKEN
Submitted by David Mason poet

This dish is a tasty, quick to prepare and, perhaps most notably, suitable for those suffering from dairy or gluten allergies (these are much more prevalent than you might first think).

The Sauce

Cut a little fresh ginger root into tiny cubes. Add three or four diced spring onions and three crushed garlic cloves. Add dry ginger (one teaspoon) and coriander (one teaspoon) and fry in a saucepan in a little olive oil for two to three minutes.

If you wish, you can add fresh lemon grass. I recommend adding fresh coriander as this gives the sauce a pleasing splash of colour.

Put about ¾ block of creamed coconut (comes in a block like margarine or butter) into a jug and add boiling water to liquefy the coconut. Add this mix slowly to the sauce until you reach the desired texture of the sauce - not too runny, not too stiff.

The sauce should be piping hot when served.

The Rice

I prefer basmati rice. Prepare this as per the instructions on the packet. It takes about ten minutes to cook.

The Chicken

Fry chicken breast cubes (2cm) in olive oil in a wok. Turn them to cook evenly. It takes about ten minutes.

The Vegetarian Option

Substitute water chestnuts for the chicken (fry in a wok).

The Serving

Put rice on the plate first, then the chicken. Pour the sauce over the top. Serve with decorations of cashew nuts, stir-fried bean sprouts and mange-tout. A few slices of roasted red pepper add extra colour.

'Lovely and creamy - knew it would be delicious!'

I have performed poetry to more than 100,000 children and adults over the last ten years. I teach poetry, drama and creative writing to pupils aged 5 to 18 years. I love my work and the students I work with. I ran a restaurant called "Alfresco" in Ludham, Norfolk, for eight years before my reincarnation. Anyone fancy a cookery-poetry workshop? There's no one better equipped to deliver!

COTTAGE PIE

Ingredients

250g Mince (we use pork, but any mince will be good)
4 Good Sized Potatoes (peeled and boiled then mashed)
2 Parsnips (peeled and boiled then mashed)
1 Tin of Tomatoes
1 Onion (chopped)
1 Carrot (chopped)
1 Red Pepper (chopped)
5/6 Mushrooms (chopped)
Mixed herbs
Garlic (crushed)
Black Pepper

Method

- Prepare the potatoes and parsnips.
- In another pan lightly cook the crushed garlic with the chopped onion.
- When soft, add chopped pepper and mushrooms with herbs.
- Cook slightly then add mince, to seal.
- Add tin of tomatoes.
- Cook for about 25mins.
- Drain and mash potatoes and parsnips, adding a little butter and milk if you choose to.
- When the meat is cooked, place in an oven proof dish and cover with the mash. (It may be necessary to strain some of the juice from the meat mixture before you put the potato mash in the top. This juice can be used as gravy).
- Add the grated cheese and toast under the grill.

Cooking Club
Arden Grove Infant and Nursery School

CHEESE AND POTATO PIE

Ingredients

4 Large or 6 Medium Potatoes to Mash.
1 Onion (chopped)
1 red pepper (chopped)
2 Rashes of Bacon (cut into small pieces)
150g Cheese (grated)
Pkt of Cheese and Onion Crisps.

Method

- Peel and boil potatoes,
- Dry fry the chopped onion, pepper and bacon.
- Grate cheese.
- When the potatoes are soft, drain and mash.
- Add some of the cheese to the onions, pepper and bacon and mix well.
- Put in dish.
- Crush crisps and mix with the rest of the cheese.
- Place onto the potato mixture and grill until crispy.

Cooking Club
Arden Grove Infant and Nursery School

A BOGGLE RECIPE FOR MUD STEW (as remembered by Swampy)
Submitted by Tom Blofeld, creator of Bewilderwood and author, and 'Swampy' also of Bewilderwood

Swampy is a Marsh Boggle who lives in the Boggle village in Bewilderwood. His main interest in food is eating it. But he is a good cook, too, even if his mum has to help him out quite a lot of the time. Swampy likes to find his own food and even catches fish for himself. He is also an expert berry finder, but tends to eat most of them while he is picking them, so his mum often asks Mildred, the crocklebog, for these.

Swampy has recently spent quite a lot of time with Tom Blofeld, teaching him some simple Boggle recipes. He says that Tom and he are quite similar really. The way you can tell is that their tummies stick out exactly the same amount.

(NB. Don't actually make this recipe to eat, it'll make you ill and you could be very sick!)

Into a large cauldron place the following:
Three large gloop's of mud (marsh mud preferably).
Two grabs of dried or preserved sedge leaves.
A fresh nettle and its roots.
The slime from one large or two small slugs (being careful not to harm the slugs).
2 pints of bog water.
As much sugar as you can find.
Stir all of this up, and season it carefully with earwig droppings. Then, after finding a friend to help carry it, drag the entire cauldron to the darkest marsh you can think of. Leave it there.

If a duller dish is required (i.e. **one you can actually cook**) then how about making the next recipe, and eating that instead.

MARSH FISHCAKES

So the right amount of stuff you'll need is:
500g Salmon (cooked in just enough water to cover it).
500g Mashed potatoes (it is okay if they aren't well mashed).
A handful of chopped fresh herbs, preferable parsley and tarragon, but you can use dill or even chives. Not all four though).
A cup of Flour.
A cup of breadcrumbs.
An Egg.
Ketchup.
Some trousers or a skirt.
(A nice variant is to use eel or pike meat and chuck in some chopped spring onions and a little cumin. If you do that then don't use tarragon. But it's a bit daring and Swampy isn't sure he'd try it!)

Take two large sliverfish (or a chunk of Salmon) and poach it in water with a sprig of thyme for 7 minutes.

Take it out and let it cool down. While it is still warm flake it into small but not tiny chunks.

Into some of yesterday's mashed potatoes throw some tangitwigs and marsh niffigrass. (You could use a bit of chopped tarragon and parsley instead but it's not as good). Add a tiny bit of salt. Then carefully mix in the fish so it doesn't all break up.

Put some flour on a plate and muddle it about with the palms of your hands. When your pinkies are nice and white, get a lump of the fishcake mixture and shape it into a ball the size of a small yo-yo. Then squish it so it is sort of flatish. After that do the rest of the mixture in the same way, so there are lots of cakes.

Wipe your hands on your trousers or skirt.

Break an egg onto a flat bowl and mix it up a bit. Then on another plate sprinkle some seedibun crumbs (breadcrumbs are excellent instead). Take your cakes and rub them gently on the floury plate, then quickly dip them into the egg and onto the breadcrumbs until they are coated.

Wipe your hands on your Mum's trousers or skirt.

Fry these in hot oil for 3 minutes a side, until golden brown. Yummy. Eat them with lashings of ketchup.

'Brilliant! This (Marsh Fishcakes, not Mud Stew!) was one of the loveliest foods I have ever tasted.'

FRUIT AND NUT MUESLI

Ingredients
500g of Oats
4 tbsp of Sunflower Oil
4 tbsp of Clear honey
100g of Dried Apricots
75g of Sultanas
50g of Chopped Nuts

Equipment
Oven, Bowl, 2 x Baking Trays, Knife and Air Tight Container

Method
- Preheat your oven to 190 Degrees Celsius.
- Mix the oats, sunflower oil and honey together in a bowl.
- Spread the mixture onto the baking trays and cook in the oven for 10 minutes until lightly toasted.
- Remove from the oven and leave to cool.
- Chop the apricots into small pieces and mix together with the chopped nuts and sultanas.
- When the oats are cool, add the apricots, sultanas and chopped nuts.
- Mix well.
- Seal in an air-tight container.

Amie Shorten
Year 3
Woodland View Junior School, Spixworth

CHEESY CHIVE AND GARLIC CHICKEN

Ingredients
Chicken Breasts
Tub of soft cheese
1 Dessertspoon Butter
1 Teaspoon Garlic Powder
1 Teaspoon Chives
1 Chicken stock cube
Grated cheese
250ml Cheese Sauce

Method
- Steam/cook chicken.
- Add creamy cheese, butter to frying pan and melt on a low heat.
- Add the garlic and chives and mix together.
- Add the cheese sauce.
- Cut the chicken.
- Sprinkle stock cube over the chicken, massage in to get flavour.
- Add chicken to the frying pan; simmer for 5 minutes, stirring occasionally.
- Serve and sprinkle with grated cheese.

Freya and Catlin Mann
Year 4
Sprowston Junior School

SMOKED MACKERAL PATE

Ingredients
225g Smoked, Peppered Mackerel Fillets
2 tsp Olive Oil
1 tbsp Mayonnaise
1 tsp Garlic Mayonnaise
½ tsp Lemon Juice (optional)

Method
- First remove the skin from the mackerel fillets.
- Split the fillets lengthways along the centre line then roughly chop and remove any stray bones.
- Put the chopped mackerel into a food processor along with the olive oil and lemon juice. Chop for 30 seconds.
- Add the mayonnaise and blend until smooth.
- Serve on thinly sliced French bread.

Also makes great sandwich filling and will keep in the fridge for 2 days

Rebecca Richardson
Year 5
Woodland View Junior School, Spixworth

FISH FINGERS AND MASH

Ingredients
Cod/Smoked Haddock/Salmon (About 500g Total)
Beaten Egg
Flour to Dip Fish into (about 50g)
3 Slices of Breadcrumbs
4 Large Potatoes to Boil and Mash
1 Tin of Mushy Peas

Method
Peel and boil the potatoes.
Slice fish into strips.
Dip the fish into the flour, then the egg and then the breadcrumbs.
Place on a lightly greased tray and place in a hot oven (180C) for about 10 minutes.
Mash the potatoes and mix with the green mushy peas.

Cooking Club
Arden Grove Infant and Nursery School

MUSHROOM SURPRISE

Ingredients
1 Large Mushroom
1 Tomato
Grated Cheese
Slice of Ham
1 Tablespoon Olive Oil
Garlic Clove
Worcester Sauce

Method
- Peel the large mushroom
- Sprinkle oil in a frying pan, put the mushroom in when oil hot.
- Add some chopped ham and sprinkle over a little Worcester sauce
- Finely chop a clove of garlic and a tomato, put into the pan and cook for 5 minutes stirring all the time.
- Serve on a plate and sprinkle grated cheese over the top.
- Serve with a salad and enjoy.

Kevin Gray
Year 6
Terrington St Clement Community School

MILLET AND VEGETABLE GRATINEE
Submitted by Helen McDermot, Presenter BBC Radio Norfolk

Helen trained for many years in music, theatre and ballet.

Helen moved into television first at Westward TV in Plymouth, then to Norwich to work as a continuity announcer for Anglia TV.

Helen soon went on to be one of the main anchors for the daily magazine "About Anglia".

She is Director of the 999 Radio Norwich station, and is also a presenter on BBC Radio Norfolk, with a daily show between 11am and 1pm.

Ingredients
4oz millet
1 pint milk
1 pint water
3 tablespoons chopped parsley
3oz butter or margarine
1 teaspoon sage
2 medium sized leeks
Grated rind and juice of ½ lemon
1 large carrot
4 celery sticks
Salt and pepper to taste
1oz 100% wholemeal flour
4oz grated cheddar cheese

Method
Cook the millet in the measured boiling water until just tender and all the water has been absorbed. Slice the leeks, grate the carrots and finely slice the celery. Melt 2oz butter in a saucepan; add the vegetables and sauté for 10-15 minutes, stirring frequently. Add the millet and stir over very gentle heat to keep it warm. Meanwhile, melt the remaining butter in a saucepan. Stir in the flour and cook for 1 minute. Stir in the milk, herbs, lemon rind and juice, and bring to the boil. Reduce heat and simmer for 2 minutes. Pour it over the vegetables and stir well. Adjust seasoning with salt and pepper. Transfer to a warmed serving dish, sprinkle with cheese, and `bubble` under a hot grill until golden brown.
Serves 4 - 6.

Comments
The contrasting flavours and textures of millet and vegetables provide a satisfying savoury dish. This is one of my favourite vegetarian dishes. I tend not to tell people what is in it - if you mention millet they assume you're going to dish up bird food! This is a tasty, filling and cheap (or should I say cheep!) recipe and can be made in advance.
(NB. The millet is a plant that is similar to grass, and the small seed from this plant can be eaten.)
'Love the texture and taste!'

ENERGY BAR
Submitted by Norwich City Football Club on behalf of the Players

A high-energy snack packed full of goodness with all the benefits of cereals, fruit and nuts.
Makes 16
100g of pecan nuts
110g of ready to eat dried apricots
150g of porridge oats
25g of rice krispies
25g of bran flakes, lightly crushed
75g of raisins
1tps of molasses syrup
150ml of light condensed milk
10 inch x6 inch rectangular baking tin pre heat oven to 180°C, 350°F gas mark 4.

Begin by toasting the pecan nuts on a baking sheet on the top shelf of the oven for seven minutes then chop them roughly. I like to have them quite well toasted as it gives a nice nutty twist to the taste. Next chop the apricots to the same size as the pecans, and then in a large bowl mix together the oats, rice krispies, bran flakes, apricots, pecans and raisins. Now, in a small saucepan, heat the molasses syrup and condensed milk until they're warm and thoroughly blended, and then pour this mixture into the bowl. Mix it well with a wooden spoon, then simply tip the mixture into the baking tin, press it down evenly all over and bake in the oven for about 25 minutes, or until golden brown. After that leave it to get quite cold. When the cereal mixture has cooled, loosen the edges with a palette knife and turn it out upside down on to a board. Carefully cut the slab into 16 pieces. Store in an airtight tin for up to two days.
This recipe is clearly a 'Premiership' one!

'It was lovely and I loved it, it was bursting with fruity flavours.'

Norwich City Football Club is now a Premier League football team. They won promotion to the top league under the guidance of Paul Lambert. The manager had only been with NCFC for 2 years but steered the club to win back to back promotions. Their top scorer last season was their Captain Grant Holt who also won the Club's Player of the Year Award. Last season was by far the best for quite a few years. Simeon Jackson scored the goal at Portsmouth which sent Norwich to the Premier League. The Club's promotion was a real team effort.

ANCIENT FAMILY PANCAKE RECIPE
Submitted by the Lord Mayor 2010-2011, Tom Dylan

My name is Tom Dylan and I was born in Manchester in 1980. A few years ago I moved to Norwich and in 2010 became the City's youngest and first Green Lord Mayor. The role of Lord Mayor is to represent the City as 'First Citizen' although I'm still not allowed to jump the queue at the Post Office! I have attended a great number of different events and met many new and interesting people.

To my shame, I'm not much of a cook, and neither is my mum. In her defence, it was made more difficult when I decided to become vegetarian, when I was about 12 years old. Since then, the one thing that she has been able to make that still delights me, are pancakes, and Shrove Tuesday (Pancake Day) is one of my favourite festivals.

She has been kind enough to share with me the recipe, below, although in truth, when she's making them it looks like she hasn't got a clue what she's doing, and they always taste different, so I wouldn't take these instructions too seriously!

Ancient family pancake recipe

Put about a pint of milk into the 'blitzer' (I think she means food processor... but not sure!)

Add one free range egg

Add cupful of flour - you can always add more, so better to put less in to start with

Add a pinch of salt, a teaspoon of baking powder (optional). If you like American style pancakes, add a teaspoon of bicarbonate of soda.

Have lemon/lime ready to squeeze on top, as well as sugar/maple syrup/honey/banana to taste.

Put a bit of butter in the frying pan. The first pancake is a 'runt' so keep it small until the pan heats up, you should use a medium to high heat. Add a bit of the mixture, wait until the bubbles are gone, then turn/flip it over, wait until golden brown underneath. Serve straight away, and then have a family row about who's having the next one. The amounts above are enough to make more than one pancake, depending on the size of the pan.

If all this goes wrong, blame my mum, as I've never tried it. ☺

(NB. A **runt** is the smallest and weakest animal of a group born at the same time.)

'Lovely and soft, but crispy at the same time!'

MEDITERRANEAN TARTLETS

Ingredients
1 Packet of Short Crust Pastry
10 Pitted Black Olives (from Greece)
½ Red Peppers (from UK)
4oz Feta Cheese (from Greece)
1 Clove Garlic (from France)
3 tbsp Sun-dried Tomato Paste (from Spain)
3 tbsp Regular Mayonnaise (from France)
2 oz Broccoli (from UK)

Method
- Pre-heat oven to 180c, 375f, gas mark 5.
- Dust board and roll out pastry thinly.
- Using floured mini tart shaper, gently, press discs into mini muffin pan or for an alternative, place the pastry into a quiche/flan dish.
- Using the food chopper (or chop up ingredients finely) chop olives, pepper and broccoli and place into a bowl.
- Crumble cheese, crush garlic and add the sun-dried tomatoes paste and mayonnaise.
- Add to the dried ingredients and mix together.
- Place into pastry cases/quiche dish into the oven and cook for 20 - 25 minutes or until the top of the tartlets are firm to the touch.

Cookery Club
Edward Worlledge Community Junior School

'Star Recipe'

This has been chosen as our favourite children's recipe.

TART OF CONFIT OF CHERRY TOMATOES WITH TOMATO AND BASIL PESTO WITH REDUCED BALSAMIC VINEGAR
Submitted by David Adlard well known Norfolk Chef

This is for 6 people

CONFIT OF CHERRY TOMATO

1. Cut the tomatoes in half - across rather than down - and put on an oven tray cut face up
2. On the cut top put a thin slice of garlic, some thyme leaves, season, dot with olive oil and dust with icing sugar.
3. Put in the oven at a very low temperature so it doesn't brown the garlic which will be bitter. I used 50°C on my oven.
4. It takes 2½ - 3 hrs when it is cooked (crinkly round the edge).

SUN-DRIED TOMATO PESTO

Ingredients

125gm sun-dried tomatoes
2 tablespoons fresh basil
2 tablespoons fresh parsley
1 tablespoon garlic
70gm pine nuts
100ml balsamic vinegar
1 dessert spoon tomato paste
120ml olive oil (roughly to make the right consistency)
50gm grated Parmesan cheese
Salt and pepper to taste

Directions

In a food processor or blender add everything apart from olive oil. Drizzle it in when your turn the machine on to make the right consistency. Should be reasonably stiff for this recipe.

David Adlard did not become a chef until he was over thirty years old. He trained at Kilburn Polytechnic. After being an under chef for several years, he got a job as an apprentice chef at the famous Connaught Hotel in Mayfair under the direction of Chef Michel Bourdin. In 1983 after more experience in France and America he opened up his restaurant in Wymondham, outside Norwich. In 1986 he achieved the first ever Michelin star in Norfolk. He writes in the EDP Norfolk Magazine. In 2005 he was presented with The Life Achievement Award at the EDP Food Award ceremony.

BASIL PESTO
Ingredients
50gm basil (the plant from my supermarket is 25gm plus)
30gm pine nuts (roasted)
30gm freshly grated parmesan
1 clove of garlic
85ml olive oil (roughly to make the right consistency)
salt and freshly ground pepper if needed

Directions
In a food processor or blender combine everything apart from olive oil. Drizzle it in to make the right consistency. Should be reasonably loose for this recipe.

Put into squeezy bottle if you have got one, otherwise use a teaspoon.

PÂTE BRISÉE (makes 450gm)
(4 tart mould 8cm x 1¼ cm)
Ingredients
250gm plain soft flour
150gm slightly soft butter
1tsp fine salt
Pinch of caster sugar
1 egg
1 tbsp milk

1. With an electric mixer add all the ingredients without the milk and work to a grainy texture.
2. Add milk and work 'til smooth.
3. Roll into a ball, and refrigerate or freeze.
Freeze the pastry you don't use.

BALSAMIC VINEGAR
Reduce a bottle to a half - put into squeezy bottle.

ASSEMBLY
Smear generously the tart with tomato basil and warm up.
Warm up the confit.
Fill up the tarts with confit and maybe some around the outside.
Using the squeezy bottle dribble the basil pesto on the tomato and round the outside make arty circles with the balsamic vinegar.
Serve.

'Crumbly pastry and delicate tomatoes means a great dish!'

SUMMER PORRIDGE WITH FRUIT
Submitted by the Leader of Norfolk County Council, Derrick Murphy

Serves 2 people for breakfast
50g good quality porridge oats
100ml apple juice
30g walnut pieces
30g dried cranberries (or other dried fruit such as sultanas or chopped-up apricots)
1 banana
200ml cold milk

The night before, put the porridge oats in a bowl and add the apple juice; stir, cover and leave to soak overnight in the fridge.

In the morning, slice the banana into rounds and mix into the porridge with the dried fruit and walnuts.

Divide into two bowls and add the milk.

If you prefer you can replace the banana with other fruit such as mango, strawberries or pear.

'Exploding with fruit- I'd like it for breakfast!'

Derrick was educated at the University of East Anglia, University of Birmingham, University of London and the Open University.
His main career was in education. Although holding degrees in a number of subjects his main interest is in history. His main sporting interest has been Rugby Union. Today his main interests are cycling, jogging, watercolour painting and writing. I keep fit by bicycle riding and running and I enjoy eating healthy foods such as vegetables, pulses and fish. I often have porridge for breakfast and this recipe is a tasty and easy alternative when the weather is warm.

MEGA MACARONI CHEESE

Ingredients
240g Macaroni
40g Low Fat Spread
40g Flour
1 Pint Semi Skimmed Milk
150g Grated Low Fat Cheddar Cheese
25g Grated Parmesan
1 Slice of Brown Bread turned into Breadcrumbs
4 Rashers of Cooked Lean Bacon (cut into chunks)

Method

- Cook macaroni for about 8 minutes in boiling water.
- Meanwhile, melt low fat spread in saucepan, then add in flour and stir for 2 minutes.
- While keeping on the heat, slowly start adding milk, and keep stirring until it mixes to a sauce.
- Add in cheddar, most of the parmesan, bacon and some of the herbs to the sauce and stir until thickened.
- Drain macaroni and put into dish to go into oven.
- Stir into cheese and bacon sauce.
- Top with breadcrumbs and the rest of the parmesan and herbs and then put under a grill for a short while until brown.

Sam Rowlands
Year 5
Woodland View Junior School, Spixworth

TUNA PASTA

Ingredients

Pasta
1 Tin of Tomatoes
1 Tin of Tuna in Brine
Bunch of Spring onions (chopped)
Red Pepper (chopped)
Mushrooms (chopped)
Small Tin of Peas and/or Sweetcorn
Herbs
50g Cheese

Method

- Put water on to boil for pasta.
- Chop vegetables and place in frying pan with a little oil, then cook until soft.
- When water boiling, add pasta.
- Put the tomatoes and herbs in a large bowl and mix.
- Strain the tuna and add to the tomato mixture.
- Add the cooked vegetables to the tomato mixture.
- Grate cheese in a separate bowl.
- Strain pasta when cooked and add to mixture with tuna and stir.
- Place in oven proof dish.
- Sprinkle with cheese.
- Grill until crispy.

Cooking Club
Arden Grove Infant and Nursery School

RED SPAGHETTI
Submitted by the Director of Children's Services, Lisa Christensen

Lisa lives with her two daughters in central Norfolk. Lisa has worked in the public sector since she began working in 1979. She moved into the Health service and spent 5 years as Director of Community Services with Bradford Community Health Trust. She re-entered local government as an Executive Director, with mixed responsibilities. She then became Director of Social Services in Lambeth, before moving to Norfolk in 2002 as Director of Social Services. She was appointed Director of Children's Services for Norfolk in 2005.

Recipe for 4 people

Ingredients
300g spaghetti
50g butter
4 or 5 tbsp tomato puree
100g grated cheese (parmesan is best)

Method
Bring a large pan of water to the boil and put a pinch of salt into it.

Put in the spaghetti. Stir it around so that it doesn't 'clump'. Bring it back to the boil and cook for as long as it says on the packet (about 12 minutes for dried spaghetti, much less if it is fresh pasta).

Drain the spaghetti in a colander and rinse with hot water. Keep this on one side. Then, turn down the heat and put the empty saucepan back on cooker and melt the butter. Stir in the tomato puree until it is all mixed in with the butter.

Then take the pan off the heat and put the spaghetti back into the pan with the tomato puree mixture. Using a wooden spoon, turn the spaghetti over and over until it is covered in the tomato puree mixture.

Serve in bowls sprinkled with the cheese (and I like to have lots of ground black pepper as well). This is lovely with a nice crisp green salad.

'Really simple to make and tastes really delicious.'

THREE COLOUR CARBONARA
Submitted by Steve Bradley, Presenter Radio Norwich

I live and work in Norwich! I host the Breakfast Show on Norwich 99.9 (weekday's 6-10am). I have been working in the media world since leaving college, as both a TV and Radio Presenter. I'm also the Norwich City Football Club Pitch Announcer on a match day - brilliant job that gives me access all areas around the ground which, for a huge Canaries fan that I am, is brilliant! I love going the gym and staying fit and healthy ... when you gym a lot it's good to keep your carbohydrate levels up which is why my recipe involves pasta.

You can knock it up in about 15 minutes and the ingredients below will feed four:

You'll need:
312g/11oz of dried rigatoni pasta
142g/5oz Savoy cabbage, finely shredded
170g/6oz smoked back bacon (ideally with the fat chopped off)
2 garlic cloves, peeled and lightly chopped
1 green chilli, deseeded and finely chopped
110g/3½oz closed cup mushrooms thinly sliced
198g/7oz frozen peas, defrosted
2 medium tomatoes deseeded and chopped
3 large egg yolks *(not advisable for pregnant ladies/elderly/babies)*
100g/3½oz quark (cheese)
Salt and freshly ground black pepper
170g/6oz sweet and crunchy salad, to serve

1)   Bring a large saucepan of lightly salted water to the boil. Add the pasta and boil for 9 minutes. Add the cabbage for the final 4 minutes
2)   Meanwhile, cook the bacon in a non-stick frying pan for 3-4 minutes. Add the garlic, chilli and mushrooms and cook for 3 minutes. Add the peas and tomatoes and cook for a minute to heat through.
3)   In a small bowl, whisk the egg yolks and quark together with some seasoning.
4)   Ladle some of the pasta cooking water into a cup, reserve and drain the remaining pasta. Place the pasta back in the saucepan. Add the bacon and vegetable mixture and stir through. Remove from the heat and stir in the egg and quark mixture, adding 2-3 tablespoon of the reserve cooking water to loosen the sauce a little.
5)   Serve with the sweet and crunchy salad.
6)   Enjoy!

'Wow! So much tastier than your average carbonara!'

BREADS

CRUSTY COB
Submitted by Galton Blackiston, Norfolk's Celebrity Chef

This recipe can be done by hand or with an electric food mixer and 'K beater' attachment

Makes 1 x 450g (1 lb) loaf

500g (1 lb 2 oz) strong white flour, plus extra for dusting
1 tbsp salt
30g (1 oz) yeast
40g (1½ oz) butter, softened
300 ml (½ pint) water

In 1979, Galton set up a stall at Rye market selling his own range of home-made cakes, biscuits and preserves. Galton abandoned his plans to be a professional cricketer, deciding instead on a career as a chef.

Galton began working in the Lake District at the renowned Miller Howe, finally working his way up to the position of Head Chef.

Galton and his wife decided to run a country hotel, Morston Hall, it is one of Britain's leading country hotels.

Galton is a well known face on cookery shows such as BBC2's Great British Menu and Saturday Kitchen.

Put the flour, salt, yeast and butter into a large bowl and mix together.
Add nearly all the water and blend the ingredients together then add the remaining water and mix in the bowl for 2 minutes.
Tip the dough out onto a lightly floured surface and knead well for 5 minutes, (or if using an electric food mixer, leave the machine running to knead the dough) then place the dough back in the bowl and leave covered with a damp cloth in a warm place to rest and rise for 2 hours.
Line a baking tray. Shape the dough into a ball, place on the baking tray and leave to rise for 1 hour.

Pre-heat the oven to 220C/425F/Gas 7.
Using a sharp knife, slash the dough across the top and dust with flour. Bake for 30 minutes until golden brown, then transfer to a wire rack to cool.

'Crunchy and crusty just like its name!'

ROSEMARY AND SEA SALT FOCACCIA

Submitted by Alison Senter of The Hero, Burnham Overy Staithe, North Norfolk

I am currently one of the owners and Chefs of The Hero in Burnham Overy Staithe. I was never a chef before working here, but seem to have a certain mad streak that makes me love this job and of course I learnt all of the important things to know about cooking from my mum - who is incidentally, fab at cooking!!
I am a past pupil of Kinsale, which was a Middle School at the time.

I think this book is a great idea and hope that it will convince all of you to get in the kitchen and make something from raw ingredients rather than buying something ready made from the supermarket.

Ingredients
* 300ml/½ pint tepid water * 1½ tsp dried yeast or 2 heaped tsp fresh yeast
* 500g/1lb 2oz '00' flour or strong white bread flour, plus extra for dusting * 1½ tsp salt * 3 tbsp olive oil, plus extra for greasing * extra virgin olive oil, for drizzling * medium coarse sea salt * 2 sprigs rosemary, torn into small pieces

Method
1. Pour a little of the tepid water into a small bowl. Add the yeast and blend using your fingers. Leave the yeast for five minutes to soften and dissolve.
2. Mix the flour and salt together in a large mixing bowl. You may like to transfer your mixture to a pastry board or other flat work surface at this stage and prepare the dough there, in traditional Tuscan style. Otherwise, mix the dough in the bowl.
3. Make a well in the centre of the flour and salt mixture. Pour the blended yeast and water into the well along with the olive oil. Mix thoroughly. Gradually add the rest of the tepid water until a sticky dough is formed.
4. Transfer the dough onto a floured surface. Gather any stray pieces. Knead the dough for about 10 minutes, adding a little extra flour if necessary, until smooth and elastic and the dough no longer sticks to your hand.
To see if it is ready, you can carry out the stretch test: pull off a piece of dough; it should be elastic enough not to break quickly when stretched out.
5. Make the dough into a nice smooth ball, should take about 5 minutes.
6. Oil a bowl and place the dough inside and cover with either oiled cling film or a damp tea towel. Leave in a warm place to rise until doubled in size - about 1½ hours depending on the room temperature.
7. Use your fist to knock it back, then knead it again for a further two minutes.

8. Leave to rest again, but only for 5-10 minutes.
9. Shape by placing into a shallow baking tray, using your hands to spread it out to a depth of about 1.5cm/¾in, then allow to rise again, covered with a tea towel, until doubled in size - this will take about 30 minutes. Preheat the oven to 200C/400F/Gas 6.
10. Create a dimpled effect by repeatedly pushing your fingertips gently into the surface of the dough. Drizzle a generous amount of extra virgin olive oil evenly over the dough. Sprinkle over the sea salt and push the small pieces of rosemary into the dough add some roasted vegetables or cherry tomatoes if you fancy it, or even some mozzarella.
11. Bake for 25-35 minutes or until the top is crusty and cooked through to the base.

Hopefully, this should turn out fine! I had a couple of attempts and decided that you can't use old yeast because the dough doesn't rise!!

If you have trouble finding fresh yeast ask in any supermarket with a bakery and they should be able to give you some.

'I'd never eaten Focaccia before; it really does taste as good as it looks!'

CHEESE AND HAM SCONES

Ingredients
50g Cold Butter
250g Self Raising Flour
150ml Milk
Pinch of Salt
75g Ham (chopped into small pieces)
75g Cheese (grated)

Method
- Preheat the oven to Gas Mark 7 or 220C.
- Lightly grease a baking tray.
- Sift flour into a large Bowl.
- Cut butter into small cubes and add to flour
- Rub the butter into the flour until it resembles breadcrumbs. Be quick so the butter doesn't melt.
- Add the ham and cheese to the mix and gently stir.
- Pour in the milk a little at a time and gently stir until you get a sticky ball of dough.
- Gently knead the dough with the palm of your hands for 1 minute.
- Sprinkle flour onto your work surface and rolling pin.
- Roll out the dough evenly to a thickness of about 2.5 cm.
- Use a pastry cutter or upside down glass to cut out your scones and place on a baking tray.
- Put tray in middle of oven and cook for approximately 25 minutes or until golden brown.
- Allow to cool before munching.
- Eat whole or sliced in half with butter.

Olivia Orford

Year 4

Woodland View Junior School, Spixworth

QUICK BREAD AND BUTTER

Ingredients
Quick Bread 3 Cups of Whole Wheat Flour
4 Teaspoons of Baking Powder
1 Teaspoon of Salt
1½ Cups of Milk
¼ Cup of Liquid Fat (e.g. vegetable/olive oil)
Quick Butter Double Cream

Method
Quick Bread:
- Mix dry ingredients.
- Mix liquids and add to dry mix.
- Stir until there is no more dry flour. (You may need a little bit more or less liquid. The dough should be moist but not sticky. It may take a few minutes for the flour to fully absorb the liquid, so don't rush to add liquid or flour to it.)
- Score lightly the surface in a diamond or X shape to prevent splitting of the crust. This is country style bread that should be sliced thick.
- It is important not to overwork the dough.
- Shape into a ball or an oval, with oiled hands.
- Sprinkle a few poppy seeds on top before baking.
- Place on clean, floured baking sheet.
- Bake for 40 minutes at 400F.

Quick Butter:
- Put the cream in a jar with a lid, and shake until blobs of butter form in the jar.
- Rinse off the liquid with fresh cold water.
- Keep mixing the butter until the water runs clear
- Eat as soon as possible!

Cookery Club
Gayton First School

BANANA LOAF
Submitted by Susan Barron, confectioner at Byfords in Holt

Ingredients
8oz/227gm Self Raising Flour
5oz/142gm Caster Sugar
4oz/113gm Sultanas
1.5oz/42gm Walnuts (chopped)
2 Eggs
12oz/340 Peeled Bananas
4oz/113gm Butter

Method
Rub the butter into the flour until it looks like breadcrumbs.
Mix in the sugar, then add the eggs & mix to a paste.
Stir in the sultanas & chopped walnuts, mix in the peeled banana.
Continue mixing until a soft mixture is obtained.
Spoon the mixture into a greased & lined 2lb loaf tin.
Bake for approximately 2hours, Gas 2, 300F, 150C.

'It was sweet and juicy, I want more of it!'

I started work as a confectioner at the age of 17, my father found the job for me. It was with a lady who had baked for all her working life, taking over the family retail bakery.
I remained there for a number of years until my first child was born. A further 3 children meant that I didn't return work for a number of years. On moving to Sheringham a number of years ago, I found employment at The Mulberry Tearooms in Sheringham, making a variety of confectionary and meals. Approximately 10 years ago I went to work for Iain & Clair Wilson at Byfords in Holt. Well things have grown beyond anything I could have imagined. Today I produce a large variety of cakes, tarts & desserts. So here I am at the age of 59 still producing products in the same way I did at 17.

SOUPS

Paul Lambert

CARROT AND CORIANDER SOUP
Submitted by Norwich City Football Club on behalf of Paul Lambert, the Manager

This recipe is one of Paul Lambert's favourite soups from the training ground, cooked by our Head Chef, **Tony Carver**. This is always good when you come in from a freezing cold training session and it really helps to warm you up!

Serves 6

2lb (900g) carrots, peeled and chopped
1 tbsp fresh coriander, roughly chopped (with stalks)
1oz (25g) butter
1 small clove of garlic, chopped
1 medium onion, chopped
2 pints (1 litre) vegetable stock
3 tbsp fresh coriander leaves, finely chopped.
3 tbsp creme fraiche
salt and freshly ground black pepper.

Heat the butter over a gentle heat; add the carrots, onions and garlic. Cook gently with a lid until softened. Next add the stock, roughly chopped coriander leaves and stalks and seasoning. Bring to the boil and simmer gently for 15-20 mins until cooked. Leave to cool a little, blend until smooth and stir in finely chopped leaves and creme fraiche. Reheat to serve, check seasoning to taste.

'Amazing! Good depth of flavour!'

A former Scottish international midfielder, Lambert took charge at Carrow Road in August 2009 and led the Canaries to the League One title during his first season in charge of the Club. As a player Lambert enjoyed an impressive career and after starting out at St Mirren he later played for Motherwell, Borussia Dortmund and Celtic before tasting management with a role as player/manager at Livingston. Before his arrival at Carrow Road the 41-year-old had also managed at Wycombe Wanderers and Colchester United. After only two years as Manager of Norwich City he has steered the club to back-to-back automatic promotions.

CARROT AND LENTIL SOUP

Ingredients
1 Onion, Peeled and Chopped
3 Carrots, Peeled and Chopped
1 oz Butter
4 oz Split Red Lentils
2 Medium Potatoes, Peeled and Chopped
2 Pints of Water
2 Chicken Stock Cubes
1 Bay Leaf
Salt and pepper (stock cubes contain salt- so go easy on the salt)

Method
- Prepare vegetables.
- Melt butter in a large saucepan and gently fry onion for about 5 minutes to soften (do not brown)
- Add potatoes and carrots. Stir, and then add water, stock cubes and bay leaf.
- Add lentils.
- Bring to the boil, cover with lid and cook gently until vegetables and lentils are soft
- Remove from heat and take out the bay leaf.
- Let the soup cool, then whizz in a processor.
- (Leave chunky if liked, will freeze well for 3 months)

Sam Roberts
Year 5
Kinsale Junior School

CHILLED YOGHURT AND MINT SOUP
Submitted by David Adlard well known Norfolk Chef

Serves 6
1 cucumber
good handful of mint
1 garlic cloves
60gm yogurt
150ml water (adults might prefer white wine!)
25ml white wine vinegar
seasoning
100ml crème fraiche

1. Peel the cucumber and scrape out the seeds in the middle with a teaspoon and throw away (compost!)
2. Cut up roughly 2-3 cm in size (reserve roughly 3cm at the ends for later) and add to blender
3. Add roughly cut up garlic without the root at the end, destalked mint, yogurt, crème fraiche, white wine, vinegar, salt and pepper
4. Process in the blender 'til smooth
5. Taste and adjust if it needs it and put in the fridge to cool down
6. Serve with small diced reserved cucumber, chives or equivalent herb and borage/nasturtium flower if it's in your garden (or any combination of herbs and flowers).

We serve a small amount for a pre-starter - it's kind of sharp and it alerts the taste buds but too much if it's a regular soup plate.

'The more I have, the more I like- really refreshing!'

CELERIAC SOUP WITH RICOTTA DUMPLINGS
Submitted by Tim Kinnard, MasterChef finalist 2010

This recipe is a dish that is similar to something I cooked when I was on MasterChef. I made it for a meal we served at the Tower of London - served in Henry 8th's bedroom!

Ingredients
1x Large Celeriac
1x Large Leek
Fresh Chicken Stock (1 litre)
1 egg
100g Ricotta Cheese
1 tablespoon grated Parmesan Cheese
2 tablespoons Plain Flour
2 tablespoons Bread Crumbs
Salt and Pepper
Butter

Method
1. Finely slice leeks and cook in large pan with butter until soft. Peel and chop celeriac into 2cm chunks and put in a pan with the leeks.
2. Add stock to the celeriac and leek mixture and cook for 20-30 minutes until the celeriac is tender.
3. Place the stock, celeriac and leeks in a blender and blend until smooth.
4. Mix together in a bowl the ricotta, parmesan, flour and bread crumbs with the egg.
5. Put the soup back in a pan and drop small balls of the ricotta dumpling mix into it. Cook the dumplings in the soup for 3-4 minutes. (Optional, we decorated with fresh parsley for the photograph)
6. Serve

'Explosion of surprising tastes!'

After reaching the finals of MasterChef 2010, Tim left the medical world behind and set up his own patisserie business Macarons & More.
Tim specialises in French Macarons and other patisserie. He sells his cakes through delis and cafes in Norfolk and on-line via
www.macaronsandmore.com
He lives in Norfolk with his young family.

BUTTERNUT SQUASH SOUP WITH CHEESEY CROUTONS

Ingredients

1 Medium size Butternut Squash
1 Onion
1 Carrot
1 Potato
2 Vegetable stock cubes or 2 teaspoons vegetable powered stock (Bouillon)
1 litre water
50g Butter
Pinch of salt
Dash of cream (optional)
2 slices of bread
100g Cheddar Cheese

Method
Soup:

- Peel the butternut squash.
- Cut in half and spoon the seeds out.
- Chop the butternut squash into small chunks.
- Peel and slice the carrot.
- Peel the potato and cut into small chunks.
- Peel and dice the onion.
- Melt the butter in a large pan, add the onion and cook until softened.
- Add the butternut squash, carrot, potato and salt.
- Add the vegetable stock and water. You may need to add more water to ensure all the vegetables are covered.
- Bring to the boil and then simmer until all the vegetables are soft.
- When the vegetables are soft, puree the soup in a blender or food processor.
- Return the soup to the pan and add a dash of cream for extra creaminess.
- Keep warm whilst making the croutons.

Cheesey Croutons:

- Grate the cheese.
- Grill both slices of bread.
- Share the cheese between the grilled bread.
- Place this under the grill until the cheese is slightly melted.
- Remove from the grill and cool slightly.
- When cooled, cut the cheesey toasted bread into chunks.

Serve the soup and place the croutons on top. Enjoy!
Serves 4 - 6.

Ella Thornhill
Year 2
Ghost Hill Infant and Nursery School

SALADS

Amelia Reynolds

TOMATO, OLIVE AND SPRING ONION COUSCOUS
Submitted by Simon Newbery, Managing Director of Orchard Toys

Personally, I detest couscous, but my wife tells me it's good for me and the tomato, olive and spring onions make it bearable! Enjoy....

Ingredients

1 litre of tomato juice
1 sprig of thyme
1 clove garlic, crushed
200 g couscous
10 black olives
3-4 spring onions
Salt and black pepper

Method

1. Place the tomato juice in a medium saucepan. Add the leaves from the thyme, and the crushed garlic, and bring to a boil. Boil vigorously, stirring occasionally, for about 20 minutes or until the volume of liquid has reduced to 500ml.
2. Place the couscous in a mixing bowl. Pour the reduced tomato juice over it and stir gently until thoroughly blended. Set aside to infuse and cool for 15-20 minutes, or longer if desired.
3. Slice the olives, removing the stones as necessary. Slice the spring onions. When the couscous has absorbed the tomato sauce, fork through the mixture delicately to separate the grains.
4. Add the olives and spring onions to the bowl and fold them in gently, then season to taste with salt and pepper. Serve warm, at room temperature, or chilled.

'Loved it, a real mix of flavours and textures.'

I have just clocked up 20 years working for Orchard Toys in the very year that the company celebrates 40 years in business. In that time I have seen the company grow from a very small concern to the household name it is today. Like all the staff here, I am very proud of what Orchard Toys has become. One of the most rewarding things I have been involved in during my time with Orchard Toys has been the development of a partnership with the Aquila Club at Kinsale Junior School.

TOMATO AND CUCUMBER SALAD

Ingredients
1 - 2 Cucumbers
2 - 3 Medium Tomatoes
Salt
Pepper
A Little Garlic, Minced
2 Tablespoons of Olive Oil
2 - 4 Tablespoons of Balsamic Vinegar
Fresh Chopped Basil (optional)

Method
- Cut tomatoes and cucumbers into small pieces.
- Place in a bowl.
- Add remaining ingredients and stir.
- Refrigerate for an hour to let flavours come together.
- Fresh chopped basil is a nice addition.

Henry Lee
Year 3
Mulbarton Junior School

SEARED TUNA WITH PUY LENTIL SALAD
Submitted by David Adlard well known Norfolk Chef

Serves 2 people

Ingredients
100g Puy lentils
30g pine kernels
1 shallot cut into small dice
1 tsp balsamic vinegar
1 tsp olive oil plus extra for drizzling
1 tsp wholegrain mustard
2 tsp chopped flat-leaf parsley (or the normal one)
Seasoning
2 x 80 gm tuna
Quite a lot of sesame seeds

Method (Tuna)
Season the tuna and cover them with sesame seeds.

Sear them in a non-stick pan with a tiny amount of oil at a high heat, 2-3 mins on each side so the seeds will be nice and brown. Put them on a baking tray and bake in the oven on 180 degrees for 15 minutes until cooked through. Leave to cool.

When cold (a fridge is better to firm the fish up), slice thinly at an angle and make a good presentation with the lentils.

Method (Lentils)
Add all the ingredients and taste.

Put the lentils in a round mould on the plate (I use 7cm x 3.5cm, fill ¾ full and press down with a spoon so when you lift it off you have a nice circle) or just use a spoon to make an arty decoration with the tuna.

'Loved the nutty lentils combined with the tuna!'

BUTTERNUT SQUASH AND GOAT'S CHEESE SALAD
Submitted by Amelia Reynolds, Presenter and Journalist BBC Look East

My name is Amelia Reynolds. I am a presenter and journalist working for BBC Look East and the Politics Show. I am married to BBC Inside Out Presenter David Whiteley and we have a baby called Annabel. My favourite food is goat's cheese ... hence the recipe I have sent you!

1/2 a butternut squash
2 large handfuls of baby Spinach leaves
1 bag of mixed salad leaves
A handful of pine nuts
Log of Goat's Cheese (I like the sort with rind)
Olive Oil
Balsamic vinegar
Salt and Pepper to taste

Peel the butternut squash... cut into chunks and put into a roasting tin. Toss in olive oil, salt and pepper. Roast in oven for 40 minutes or until tender and slightly browned (180 C).
Meanwhile in a bowl mix the spinach leaves and salad leaves
Add cooled butternut squash and goat's cheese (cut into chunks)
Dress with olive oil and balsamic vinegar, salt and pepper
Sprinkle with pine nuts
Serve with warm ciabatta bread for a healthy lunch.

'Really delicious- butternut squash, pine nuts and goats cheese = excellent combination!'

FRESH SALMON SALAD

Ingredients

Four 65g Salmon Fillets
One Iceberg Lettuce (Shredded)
Half a Cucumber, Finely Sliced
100g Strawberries, Hulled and Sliced
450g New Potatoes, Scrubbed, Boiled and Halved
300ml Sour Cream
4 tblsp of Chopped Fresh Mint
Salt and Freshly Ground Black Pepper
4 tsp Raspberry Vinegar

Method

- Place the salmon fillets in a large pan and cover with cold water.
- Bring to the boil and simmer for 4 minutes, then turn off the heat.
- Leave in the liquid for 10 minutes, then remove and cool.
- Leave to chill in the fridge.
- Place the lettuce onto 4 serving plates and arrange a ring of cucumber around each one. Place the salmon fillet onto the lettuce.
- Mix the potato, sour cream and mint, then season.
- Spoon a little potato mixture around each fillet.
- Drizzle the raspberry vinegar over the lettuce, cucumber and strawberries and serve immediately.
- This is enough to serve 4.

Isabel Harmer-Borley
Year 4
Grimston Junior School

BISCUITS AND CAKES

Phil Gormley

SHEILA'S HEALTHY FRUITY FLAPJACKS

Submitted by the Chair of the Board of the National Health Service, Norfolk, Sheila Childerhouse

This recipe involves heating up food on a stove and baking in an oven. It is great fun to do but you will want an adult to help you to make sure you stay safe! My grandchildren love flapjacks and I am sure you will love these too.

Switch on an oven to 170C/Gas Mark 4.

Then you will need to find:

Ingredients
- 250g porridge oats
- 150g olive oil spread
- 5 cereal spoons runny honey
- 9 dried apricots, cut into small pieces
- $\frac{1}{2}$ large eating apple, chopped small or grated
- 1 banana, chopped into small pieces

Method
1. Gently melt the olive oil spread and honey together in a saucepan over a medium heat, but don't let it get too hot and bubble. You will want an adult to help you with this.
2. Remove the pan from the heat.
3. Add the oats, apricots, apple and banana and mix together well (you can really mash the banana in well!).
4. Press the mixture into a tin measuring 15cm x 25cm and make sure it is spread evenly. The tin does not need to be exact, but try not to allow the mixture to be too thin.
5. Put into the pre-heated oven for about 20-30 minutes.
6. You may want to check it after 15 or 20 minutes, because when it is golden brown, you need to take it out. Making sure to use oven gloves to protect your hands. An adult can help you with this. Then cut the warm mixture into squares in the tin.
7. You can put the tin on a cooling rack to help it cool faster.
8. When it is cool, cut the flapjacks again and get them out to cool further before they are ready to eat. Enjoy!

You can always try putting different types of fruit in - blueberries are delicious and extremely good for you. Or dried fruit such as raisins and cranberries.

'It was really lovely and it was sweet, I would buy it again!'

Apart from being a mum and a grandmother, I am Chair of the Board of NHS Norfolk. We spend £1.2 billion a year to provide NHS care in Norfolk! Our job is to work out what sort of health services the people of Norfolk need and then make sure we have the right hospitals, doctors, nurses and medicines, ready whenever you need them. So my days are spent meeting with people, making sure that the NHS looks after patients in the best way possible. When I'm not working I enjoy walking, cycling gardening and playing with the three grandchildren!

WHOLEMEAL CARROT AND COURGETTE ROCK CAKES

Ingredients
60g Self Raising Flour
60g Wholemeal Self Raising Flour
60g Margarine
60g Caster Sugar
50g Grated Carrot
50g Grated Courgette
50g Sultanas
Cinnamon to personal taste (optional)
½ Beaten Egg

Method
- Place flours in mixing bowl, stir to combine.
- Rub in margarine.
- Stir in sugar.
- Add grated carrot, courgette sultanas and cinnamon (if using).
- Add enough egg to make stiff dough.
- Place spoonfuls onto greased baking sheet (amount depends on size).
- Bake for 15-20 minutes till golden. 180-200 Celsius.

Lily Strike
Year 5
Lionwood Junior School, Norwich

RICE CRISPIE CAKES

Ingredients
Cake
200g White Chocolate
200g Rice Crispies
Bun Cases
DecorationCherries
Strawberry Lace Sweets
Chocolate Buttons
Raisins

Method
- Break chocolate up and put into a glass bowl over simmering water, stir until melted.
- Take off the heat and add the rice crispies and stir well.
- Put a spoonful of mixture in each bun case.
- To decorate make ears out of the chocolate buttons and attach to mixture, cherries as a nose, raisins as the eyes and the strawberry laces as a tail and whiskers.
- Allow to set.

Liam Schrier

Year 1

Terrington St Clements Community School

TOSS IN FRUIT CAKE

Submitted by the Acting Chief Executive of the East Anglian Air Ambulance, Steve Whitby

As acting Chief Executive of the EAAA I am responsible for all aspects of the Charity's work. This includes raising funds (we get no direct government or National Lottery support), making sure we have helicopters and pilots 365 days a year and also ensuring that our doctors and paramedics have all the equipment they need. In the last 10 years ago we have flown over 10000 missions across East Anglia and with the support of people like the Aquila Club at Kinsale Junior School we will be able to continue for many years to come.

My special thanks for donating your profits to the air ambulance - we are very grateful.

Ingredients

8oz self raising flour
4oz sugar
12oz dried fruit
2oz glace cherries
½ teaspoon mixed spice
2 eggs
4 fluid oz milk
4 fluid oz sunflower oil
½ teaspoon almond essence
Demerara Sugar (to sprinkle on top)

Method

Mix all the ingredients (except the Demerara Sugar) together thoroughly
Pour into an 8 inch cake tin
Sprinkle Demerara Sugar on top
Bake in the middle of the oven at 180 degrees c. For 1 hour 15 minutes
Half way through cooking turn the cake round to ensure it cooks evenly.

'It was a fruity burst in my mouth: I will never find anything like it!'

MILK CHOCOLATE CAKE

Ingredients

4oz Margarine
7oz Self Raising Flour
8oz Sugar
2oz Cocoa Powder
Pinch of Salt
5 Tablespoons Evaporated Milk
5 Tablespoons Water
2 Eggs

Method

- Heat oven to Gas mark 5 or 190C.
- Grease and line two sandwich tins.
- Rub together the margarine with all the dry ingredients until it resembles breadcrumbs.
- Beat eggs with the liquid ingredients and add to breadcrumb mixture, stirring continuously.
- Divide mixture evenly between the tins and level top with a knife.
- Bake on middle shelf for approximately 35 minutes until they are well risen and beginning to shrink away from the sides.
- Sandwich together with buttercream and dust the top with icing sugar.

Bethany Lester
Year 4
Woodland View Junior School, Spixworth

GIANT JAFFA CAKE

Ingredients
1 Packet of Orange Jelly
375ml Orange Juice
275g Chocolate
300ml Double Cream
25cm Sponge Flan Case

Method
- Boil orange juice.
- Pour into a jug & melt jelly.
- Line the cake tin with cling film.
- Pour jelly & orange juice into the flan case when cool.
- Melt the chocolate & half the cream over water and leave to cool.
- Wipe the rest of the cream in peaks & fold into chocolate.
- Don't set!
- Place jelly into flan case.
- Leave to set for at least 30 minutes.
- Sprinkle with chocolate.

Kayleigh Gare
Year 4
Mulbarton Junior School

NANNY'S 'SMARTIES' SHORTBREAD

Ingredients
250g Plain Flour
90g Caster Sugar
175g Butter/Margarine
'Smarties'

Method
- Preheat the oven to around 180C.
- Mix ingredients together in a large bowl.
- Bring together to form a dough (add a drop of water if needed to bind altogether).
- Roll out to 1cm thickness on a floured surface.
- Cut into rounds or whatever shapes you wish.
- Press a couple of 'Smarties' into each shortbread.
- Place on a baking paper covered baking tray.
- Bake in oven until just turned golden on top.
- Allow to cool, eat and enjoy!!

Cookery Club
Gayton First School

PEAR AND ALMOND CAKE
Submitted by the Eastern Daily Press 'Chef of the Future' 2010, Hannah Rowberry

This is a lovely moist cake and works well either as a teatime cake or a dessert if you serve it with ice cream or creme fraiche! It's a great healthy cake as it contains no fat, no flour (so it's **gluten and dairy-free**) and is has a low sugar content as it contains pear puree for a natural sweetness...although after all that I promise that it tastes totally gorgeous!

Ingredients
3 large Pears (Comice or Williams are ideal)
1 tbsp Lemon juice
8 free-range eggs
325g ground almonds
275g Fairtrade caster sugar
1 tbsp lemon juice
50g flaked almonds

Method
- Pre-heat the oven to Gas mark 4 or 180oC.
- Peel, core and roughly chop the pears and place in a small saucepan. Add the lemon juice and cook over a gentle heat until the pears are very soft and mushy. Remove from the heat and allow to cool slightly.
- Put the pears into the bowl of a free-standing electric mixer and whizz to a puree. Add the eggs, sugar, ground almonds and lemon juice and blitz until the mixture is a smooth batter.
- Pour the mix into a 10 inch springform cake tin (a tin in two parts) which has been lined with greaseproof paper and lightly greased round the edges and bottom. Sprinkle the flaked almonds over the top and bake in the oven for approximately 45 minutes until firm and a skewer inserted in the middle comes out clean.
- Leave to cool in the tin before releasing, cutting into slices and enjoying!

'Lovely texture and not too sweet, loved the almonds!'

Hannah Rowberry is a qualified pastry chef and runs her own bespoke celebration cake business in Norwich. She trained at Gordon Ramsay at Claridge's in 2008 alongside studying a Diploma in Patisserie at Westminster College in London. Hannah was delighted to win Chef of the Future 2010 in the EDP food awards and set up Honeysuckle Cakes shortly after to pursue her passion for creating unique cakes and confectionary for any occasion.

hannah@honeysucklecakes.co.uk

BANANA MUFFINS

Ingredients

175g Plain Flour
1 Teaspoon Baking Powder
75g Sugar
3 Ripe Bananas
1 Tablespoon Cornflour
50g Margarine
2 Eggs

Equipment

2 Large Mixing Bowls, 2 Bun Trays, Tablespoon, Teaspoon, 2 Forks, Palette Knife, Electric Whisk, Plate, Sieve, Greaseproof Paper, Measuring Jug, Cooling Rack and Scales

Method

- Turn on oven - Gas 4 / 180oc.
- Grease the bun trays.
- Put flour, cornflour and baking powder into bowl and sieve together.
- Place sugar and margarine into a bowl and beat together using an electric whisk.
- Crack eggs into a jug.
- Whisk eggs using a fork.
- Add egg a little at a time to the margarine mixture and beat with electric whisk. Add some more egg, a little at a time. Beat again.
- Mash bananas with a fork, add to mixture and stir.
- Add flour to banana mixture and stir well.
- Spoon the mixture, using a teaspoon, into the bun trays and put in the oven.
- Bake for 20 minutes.
- Take muffins out of bun trays and leave to cool on cooling rack.

Key Stage 3 Pupils
John Grant School, Caister On Sea

ROCKY ROAD

Submitted by Alison Senter of The Hero, Burnham Overy Staithe, North Norfolk

Ingredients

* 250g/9oz dark chocolate, chopped * 150g/5oz milk chocolate, chopped
* 175g/6oz butter, softened, plus extra for greasing * 4 tbsp golden syrup * 200g/7oz amaretti biscuits
* 10oz mixed dried fruit and nuts of your choice (I used macadamia nuts and dried cranberries!)
* 125g/4oz mini marshmallows

Method

1. Place the dark and milk chocolate pieces into a heavy-based pan. Add the butter and golden syrup and cook over a low heat to melt and combine.
2. Place the amaretti biscuits into a freezer bag and bash with a rolling pin to make crumbs of various sizes.
3. Chop the nuts and fruits into small chunks and add to the chocolate with the mini marshmallows. Fold the mixture carefully to coat all of the solid ingredients with the syrupy chocolate mixture.
4. Pour the mixture into a 25cm/10in x 30cm/12in greased and lined baking tray and smooth the surface as much as possible (although it will look bumpy).
5. Refrigerate for two hours, or until firm enough to cut. Remove the block of rocky road from the tray and cut into 24 rectangles.

You can add all sorts of things to rocky road such as changing the dried fruits and nuts or change the chocolate to all milk chocolate or white chocolate and how about using crushed shortbread or hobnobs instead of amaretti biscuits and perhaps use Turkish delight chopped up instead of the marshmallows. I confess, I do tend to make it up as I go!

'Seriously delicious, just knowing when to stop eating them is the dilemma! As it's a 'healthy cookbook' we'd better recommend you have just a couple of rectangles at a time!'

WEETABIX CAKE
Submitted by the Sheriff of Norwich 2010-2011, Derek James

This is the Sheriff's first ever attempt at baking a cake!

Ingredients

One crumbled Weetabix
Quarter of a pint (150ml) of brown sugar
Quarter of a pint (150ml) of sultanas.
Quarter of a pint of milk
Half a pint (300ml) of self-raising flour

Method

Place first four ingredients into a bowl and leave to stand for one hour.
Stir in self-raising flour.
Pour mixture into 1lb loaf tin (greased).
Bake for 45 minutes to one hour 180 degrees C (350F) gas mark 4.
This cake is delicious eaten on its own or spread with butter/margarine.

'So tasty! I could eat the whole cake!'

Derek James was the Sheriff of Norwich during 2010/2011. He has written a column in the Norwich Evening News for 25 years. He lives in the city with his wife Bridgette and their dog Doris.
www.eveningnews24.co.uk
www.edp24.co.uk
www.letstalk24.co.uk

HEALTHY BANANA BUNS
Submitted by Becky Jago, Presenter ITV Anglia

My recipe is one that I've adapted slightly from a baby cookbook, and one I've cooked for my boys since they were tiny. They are very yummy and actually, because they have no added sugar, are quite healthy too!

Ingredients;
90g / 3 1/2 oz softened butter.
2 ripe mashed bananas
1 beaten egg
85ml / 3fl oz milk
1 tbsp runny honey
200g / 7oz self-raising wholemeal flour
2 tbsp crushed sunflower and pumpkin seeds (optional)
¼ tsp baking powder
90g / 3 1/2 oz sultanas or chopped apricots

Icing;
120g / 4oz cream cheese
1 tbsp runny honey
1 tsp lemon or orange juice

Pre-heat oven to 180C / 350F / gas mark 4.
Line the bun tray with paper cake cases (I use about 12).
Cream together the butter and bananas.
Mix in the egg, milk and honey.
Fold in the flour, baking powder, sultanas and crushed sunflower and pumpkin seeds (if using them).
Divide the mixture between the paper cases and put in the over for about 15 minutes - make sure they are golden on top.
Cool before decorating.

Icing;
Mix all ingredients together to make a smooth paste and put on top!

'Brilliant! The icing was amazing, smooth and silky! The bun was so soft!'

Becky Jago is a British television news presenter, currently employed by ITV Anglia. Jago started her media career at Vibe FM radio station 105-108, now known as Kiss 105-108, working her way up from researcher to become the co-presenter on the breakfast show. She then became the Anglian News weather girl. In November 2001, she joined the BBC's children's news program *News round*, becoming one of the two main presenters.
Becky returned to Anglia News in May 2005 as a feature reporter and presenter. She is now the main presenter of Anglia Tonight.

JAMMY OAT BARS

Ingredients
150g Self Raising Flour
85g Rolled Oats
115g Soft Butter/Margarine
150g Soft Brown Sugar
¼ Teaspoon Baking Powder
⅛ Teaspoon Salt
Jar of Strawberry Jam

Method
- Preheat the oven to around 200C.
- Mix all the ingredients except the jam, until they look like breadcrumbs.
- Place most of this mixture in a baking paper lined baking tray and press down with the back of a spoon.
- Spread a thick layer of the jam over this base.
- Take whatever of the dry mix is left, spread it over the jam layer in the baking tray and press it down lightly.
- Place in oven and bake for 25 minutes or so until a golden colour.
- Take from the baking tray and allow it to cool for at least 15 minutes.
- Cut into squares and enjoy eating!

Cookery Club
Gayton First School

FRUITY, HONEY, OATY BUNS

Ingredients
4 oz Self Raising Flour
1 Teaspoon Baking Powder
2.5 oz Margarine
4 oz Oats
1 Egg
3 Desert Spoons Honey
2 Desert Spoons Lemon Juice
2 oz Dried Mixed Fruit

Method
- Preheat oven at gas mark 5.
- Rub together flour, baking powder and margarine to make breadcrumbs.
- Add all the other ingredients and mix well, add a little milk if the mixture is too dry or stiff.
- Spoon mixture into 12 bun cases.
- Bake for 20 minutes gas mark 5 or until firm on top, the buns should be crisp on top and soft in the middle.
- Makes 12 buns.

Imogen Allen
Year 4
Woodland View Junior School, Spixworth

CHOCOLATE SHORTBREAD

Ingredients
170g (6oz) Plain Flour
60g (2oz) Corn Flour
30g (1oz) Cocoa Powder
180g (6oz) Unsalted Butter
90g (3oz) Sugar

Method
- Pre-heat the oven to 180.c/350.f/gas mark 4.
- Mix the flour, corn flour, cocoa and sugar, then work in the butter to give a soft dough.
- Roll mixture into a ball.
- Wrap in cling film, chill for half an hour.
- Grease a tin.
- Roll mixture and cut into shapes.
- Lay on baking tray
- Prick with a fork.
- Bake for 10-12 minutes.
- Leave to cool on a tray.

Claire Mellor

Year 4

Grimston Junior School

PINEAPPLE BROWNIE

Ingredients
(Dairy & egg free)
2 3/4 Cups of Plain Flour
1 1/2 Cups of Sugar
1 Tsp Baking Powder
1 Cup of Water (or use the juice from the pineapple)
1 Cup Sunflower or Vegetable Oil
1 tsp Vanilla Essence
1 Medium Tin of Pineapple Chunks

Method
- Mix all dry ingredients in a large bowl using a wooden spoon, then add all of the liquid ingredients and mix together until smooth.
- Finally add the pineapple chunks.
- Grease a baking tray, pour the mixture into the tray and put in oven to cook. Oven temperature at 175C
- Cook for 25-30 minutes.
- When it is cooked you can sprinkle over icing sugar, cut into slices and serve.

Nancy Evans

Year 4

Terrington St Clements Community School

COFFEE AND WALNUT CAKE
Submitted by the Chief Constable of Norfolk Police, Phil Gormley

Ingredients
175g soft margarine
175g caster sugar
175g self raising flour
1 tsp baking powder
3 large eggs
Handful of walnuts
Coffee

Method
Lightly grease two 18cm sandwich tins and the bases with greaseproof paper.
Beat eggs and dissolve 2 heaped tsps of instant coffee into eggs.
Put all the ingredients into a large bowl, beat well for 2 minutes. Divide mixture between the two tins.
Bake in oven for 20 minutes 180°c.
Remove from oven and allow to cool.

Make butter cream icing:

- 100g soft butter
- 225g icing sugar
- 2 heaped tsps instant coffee dissolved in a drop of water

Cream it together
Spread half between the two sponges and half on top of the cake, decorate with walnuts.

'Yum, yum, yum: topping + cake = scrumptious!'

Phil Gormley began his policing career in Thames Valley Police in 1985, working in uniform and detective roles up to the rank of Superintendent. During his career Mr Gormley has worked in varying roles, in several different police forces around the Country. In January 2010 he was appointed Chief Constable of Norfolk Constabulary.

PEAR, GINGER AND BLUEBERRY ECCLES CAKES

Ingredients
1 x 500g Pack of Puff Pastry
2 x Pears, Peeled, Cored and Chopped
75g Blueberries
1 tsp Ground Ginger
½ tsp Mixed Spice
5 Tbsps Demerara Sugar
4 Tbsps Butter
1 Egg Beaten

Method
- Over a medium heat, melt the butter and half the sugar in a saucepan.
- Add the pears, ground ginger and mixed spice.
- Cook for 5 minutes until the pears are coated and soft.
- Remove from the heat and stir in the blueberries.
- On a floured surface, roll out the pastry to the thickness of a one pound coin.
- Using a saucer or a small plate, cut out 8 circles.
- Place a tablespoon of your fruity filling in the middle of each circle.
- Fold over the edges like a parcel and pinch the edges of the pastry together.
- Turnover and flatten slightly, then place on a lightly greased oven tray.
- Use a sharp knife to cut 2 slits in the top of each Eccles Cake. (Don't go too close to the edge!)
- Brush with the beaten egg and sprinkle with the remaining sugar.
- Cook in a preheated oven at 220C or Gas Mark 7 for 20 minutes or until golden.
- Allow to cool and enjoy either warm with custard or cold with a cup of tea.

Joshua Lovett
Year 4
Woodland View Junior School, Spixworth

AUNTIE DOT'S COCONUT COOKIES

Ingredients

Base

- 3 oz Margarine
- 4 oz Granulated Sugar
- 1 tsp Vanilla Essence
- 6 oz Plain Flour
- 1 tsp Baking Powder
- 2 Egg Yolks

Top

- 2 Egg Whites
- 4 oz Desiccated Coconut
- 6 oz Caster Sugar

Method

Base:

- Cream the sugar and margarine together.
- Add egg yolks and vanilla essence and beat in thoroughly.
- Add the flour and baking powder a little at a time, stirring after each addition until the mixture is stiff and pulls together.
- Press base mixture into the bottom of a very lightly greased baking tin (approx 11 x 7 inches).

Top:

- Whisk egg whites until stiff.
- Add the caster sugar and coconut and gently fold into the egg whites.
- Spread over the top of the base.
- Bake in the centre of a pre heated oven at 350F/Gas 4/ 180C for 30-35 minutes.
- Cut into fingers, allow to cool, remove from tin and enjoy.

Luke Calcutt
Year 4
Terrington St Clement Community School

BANANA CAKE
Submitted by Norwich City Football Club on behalf of the Players

Ingredients
Two large bananas, the riper the better, peeled
and roughly chopped.
250g of self-raising flour
100g of Flora margarine
125g of caster sugar
Optional:
Handful of chocolate chips or a handful of still frozen blueberries/raspberries. A cake tin measuring 6 x 10 inches and lined with baking paper.

Pre-heat the oven to gas mark 5, 375°F (190°C).

Method
Sift the flour into a large bowl. Mix in the margarine until the mix resembles breadcrumbs. This part can be done in a food processor. Stir in the sugar and banana, plus the chocolate or fruit if using. At this stage the mix will appear quite coarse; this is perfectly normal. If the mix seems a little too dry you can mix a little milk to soften. Spoon mix into a cake tin, place in middle of a pre-heated oven for approx 30 minutes until firm and golden.
Leave in tin until cool, then slice into 12 pieces. Best eaten on the same day.

This is how the players have their Banana Cake. For a less 'athletic' version with a creamy topping see the Banana and choc Chip slice recipe at www.deliaonline.com

This recipe is clearly another 'Premiership' one!

'It was very yummy in my tummy!'

YUMMY YOGHURT MUFFINS

Ingredients
1 x Pot of Yoghurt (choose your favourite flavour, if you use corner one, save the corner to decorate your yoghurt)
Oil (sunflower or corn)
Caster Sugar
Self Raising Flour
1 x Egg

Equipment
Mixing Bowl, Wooden Spoon, 12 Case Muffin Tray (muffin cases if metal) and a
Cooling Rack

Method
- Pre-heat oven to 180 degrees C, Gas mark 4 or 375 degrees F.
- Empty yoghurt into mixing bowl (you then use the pot to measure the rest of your ingredients).
- 1 x yoghurt pot of oil poured into bowl.
- 1 x yoghurt pot of castor sugar poured into bowl.
- 3 x yoghurt pot of self raising flour poured into bowl.
- Add the egg.
- Mix all the ingredients roughly together in the bowl and then divide between the 12 muffin cases.
- Put in pre-heated oven for about 20 minutes or until firm to touch.
- Place on cooling rack until cooled.

Toby Pearce
Year 4
Belfry CE VA Primary School

DESSERTS

Chloe Smith

BANANA CHEESECAKE

Ingredients
200g Digestive Biscuits
50g Unsalted Butter
3 Bananas (very ripe)
75g Icing Sugar
400g Soft Cheese (low fat)

Method
- Grease a round baking tin (loose bottom tin is best).
- Melt the butter and leave to cool.
- Crush the digestive biscuits in a bowl.
- Stir the melted butter into the biscuits until all the pieces are covered.
- Tip mixture into the baking tin and push down flat.
- Mash the 3 bananas in a bowl, sift in the icing sugar and add the low fat soft cheese.
- Mix all these ingredients together.
- Pour the banana mixture into the baking tin on top of the biscuit base.
- Put in the fridge to set for at least 3 hours.

Ben Pummell

Year 1

Ghost Hill Infant and Nursery School

FRUIT KEBABS WITH RASPBERRY SAUCE

Ingredients
100g each of 3 - 5 different items of your favourite fruit that can be cut into chunks.
(Suggestions include: strawberries, apples, pineapple and kiwis)
150g Reduced Sugar Seedless Raspberry Jam.
1-2 tbsp Water
Large Cocktail Sticks.

Method
- Prepare your chosen fruit by peeling, coring and chopping into bite size chunks as necessary.
- Carefully spear your fruit onto cocktail sticks making sure you have some of each fruit on each stick.
- Arrange the kebabs on a serving plate.
- To make the sauce, warm the jam on a low heat with a tablespoon or two of water, stirring gently to combine.
- Put the sauce in a bowl and serve with the kebabs.
- Serves two to three people.

Madeline Wright

Year 4

Mulbarton Junior School

UPSIDE-DOWN PINEAPPLE PUDDING

Submitted by the Chairman of Broadland District Council 2010-2011, Tom Gasson

You make this pudding upside - down with the fruit topping at the bottom of the dish.
You turn it over after it has been cooked.
You should serve the pudding warm and it is especially nice served with ice cream; warm custard or cream.

Equipment: You will need:
A large mixing bowl
An 8" Ovenproof dish.
A wooden spoon
A sieve
A flat knife or large spoon

For the topping: You will need:
25 g of butter
400g tin of pineapple rings
Glacé cherries
50g brown sugar

For the sponge: You will need:
100g of self-raising flour
2 eggs
100g of caster sugar
100g of soft margarine

To make the sponge:
Turn the oven on to gas mark 4, 180 degrees C, OR 350 degrees F.
Sift the flour into a large mixing bowl.
Add the eggs, margarine and caster sugar.
Stir all the ingredients together with a wooden spoon until you have a smooth, creamy mixture.

To make the topping:
Grease the sides of a baking dish.
Melt the butter and pour it over the bottom of the baking dish so the whole bottom of the dish is covered.
Sprinkle the brown sugar evenly over the melted butter; you can use a teaspoon or your fingers to make sure that the sugar is spread evenly.
Drain the pineapple rings.
Place the first pineapple ring in the centre of the dish, then arrange the rest of the pineapple rings all around. You can use half rings if there isn't enough room to lay out all of the rings from the tin.
Next place the cherries in the centre of the pineapple rings and in any spaces to make a nice pattern.
Spread the sponge mixture over the fruit, using a knife or back of a spoon to smooth the top.
Bake on the middle shelf of the oven for 45 minutes.
Gentle loosen the edges of the pudding with a knife, then turn the pudding upside-down onto a plate.

I am Councillor Tom Gasson, Chairman of Broadland District Council. Being a Councillor means that I am an elected member of Broadland District Council. In total, I have served on the Council for seventeen years. One of my main duties is to Chair the meetings of the Council. These are the meetings where the Councillors make decisions about Council business, such as setting budgets and planning services.

'It was the tastiest thing I'd ever tasted, sweet and sticky- very delicious!'

BERRY BASH

Ingredients
Berry Mix
750g Berries
225g Caster Sugar
200ml Boiling water
Ice Cream
25g Berries
2 Vanilla Pods
500ml Double Cream
70g Sugar
3 Egg Yolks
Garnish
Drizzle of cream and a berry

Equipment
A bowl carrying 1400ml, saucepan, freezer, kettle, wooden spoon, knife, whisk, sieve, bowl, freezer proof container.

Method
Berry Mix:
- Firstly, chop any large berries to the size of approximately a two pence piece.
- Then, pour 200ml of water into a kettle and boil.
- Next, pour it into a saucepan and add the sugar.
- Stir and wait till the sugar dissolves.
- After that, add the berries and continue to stir until they soften.
- Leave to cool.
- Line your bowl with Clingfilm before pouring the mixture into it.
- Place in the freezer to freeze over night.

Ice Cream:
- Halve the vanilla pods length ways scrape out the seeds.
- Add the pods to the cream and bring to boil.
- Add the sugar and stir until the sugar has dissolved.
- Meanwhile, whisk the egg yolk in a large bowl then slowly whisk in the hot cream mixture.
- Pour the mixture through a fine sieve into another bowl, then slowly whisk in the hot cream mixture.
- Pour the mixture into a freezer proof container and freeze for 2-3 hours, or until set.

Finish:
- Take the berry mixture out of the freezer (when it's been frozen overnight) and scoop a hole out the middle.
- Mix your ice cream with the berries (quantity shown on ice cream ingredients).
- Fill the hole with the ice cream.
- Either put it back in the freezer, or pop it out of the bowl and garnish with a drizzle of cream & a berry & enjoy!

Olivia Lark and Jemima Kerkham
Year 6
Sprowston Junior School

MY MUM'S BREAD AND BUTTER PUDDING

Ingredients

6 Rounds of Brown Bread
50g Margarine
50g Demerara Sugar
Cup of Raisins and Sultanas
Cup of Pecans or Walnuts
2 Eggs
1 tbsp Golden/Maple Syrup
2 Pinches Mixed Spice
1 tsp Almond Oil
Icing Sugar (to dust)
Loaf Tin (lined)

Method

- Whilst in cup, soak fruit in boiling water.
- Butter bread on both sides and break into small pieces, then put in a mixing bowl.
- Add sugar and eggs.
- Add nuts, syrup, spice and almond oil.
- Add the fruit that was in the water. The fruit should now be soft and swollen.
- Using an electric mixer, mix until it has the same texture as a fruit cake. Place in lined tin and put in the oven for 40 minutes on 210c.
- Can be eaten cold or served with cream as a pudding.

Isaac Long
Year 1
Arden Grove Infant and Nursery School

MISSISSIPPI MUD PIE

Submitted by the Member of Parliament (MP) for Norwich North, Chloe Smith

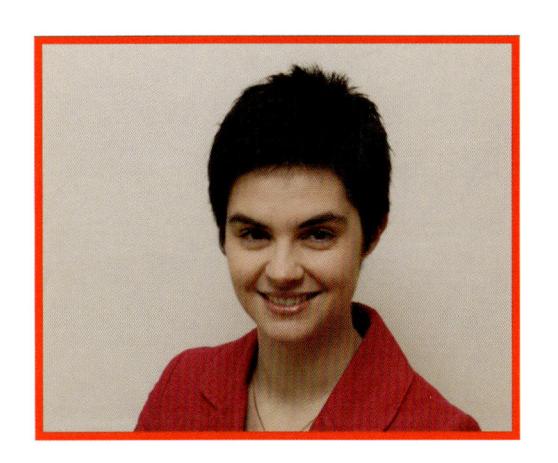

Ingredients
2oz (50g) caster sugar
4oz (100g) Self Raising flour
2oz (50g) butter or margarine
1oz (25g) plain chocolate
1/4 pint milk
1 teasp vanilla essence
4oz (100g) brown sugar
2 tablesp cocoa
1/2 pint cold water

Method
Carefully melt chocolate and butter in a bowl over a pan of hot water.
Remove bowl from pan as soon as chocolate and butter have melted.
Add caster sugar, flour and vanilla essence to this mixture and then beat in the milk.
Pour into a greased ovenproof dish.
Mix brown sugar and cocoa and spread on top of pudding mix.
Slowly pour 1/2 pint cold water over the top of the mixture.
It looks disastrous but pour gently and it will be fine!
Bake in oven for about 45 minutes at gas mark 4/350F/180C.
The pudding should feel springy to the touch when pressed lightly.
The 'mud' will have sunk to the bottom!

'Get stuck in- my favourite! Yum yum!'

I'm the Member of Parliament for Norwich North, which includes Hellesdon. I represent local people's views and needs in Westminster, where laws are made for the UK. I'm a Norfolk girl and I live in Norwich. I most enjoy the work I do at home in Norwich - when I'm not required to be present in Parliament, from Monday to Thursday most weeks - because then I can make sure I get around to meet and talk to as many people as possible in schools like Kinsale Junior School and in all sorts of other places.

FRUIT SALAD

Ingredients

20 Grapes
2 Apples
2 Oranges
2 Kiwis
11 Strawberries
1 Melon
2 Pears

Method

- Wash all the fruit.
- Chop up your fruit.
- Put fruit in a bowl.
- Get your orange juice and water, mix them.
- Eat it!

Georgia Newman
Year 1
Arden Grove Infant and Nursery School

DRINKS

The Hero

MANGO, STRAWBERRY AND COCONUT SMOOTHIE

Submitted by Alison Senter of The Hero, Burnham Overy Staithe, North Norfolk

You can make a smoothie out of just about any fruit, so try some different versions of your own!!!
Here is one I made which served 2/3 people

Ingredients

1 Ripe Mango
1 Ripe Banana
Small punnet of strawberries
5 tbsp tablespoons of coconut cream
Ice cubes (optional)

Method

Just blend all of the ingredients together and put it in a glass! Job done, yummy!
If you think it's not sweet enough, add a spoon of honey!
If it's too thick add a small amount of mango juice or milk.

'This is really fantastically yummy; the problem is knowing when to stop drinking it!'

FRUIT SMOOTHIE

Ingredients
You decide the amounts you want using these ingredients!
Strawberries
Raspberries
Grapes
Orange
Vanilla Ice Cream
Strawberry Ice Cream.
Yogurt
Method
- Mix it all together using a blender.

Maggie Carey
Year 1
Arden Grove Infant and Nursery School

BEAUTIFUL BLUE BLISS

Ingredients
Banana (whole)
Blueberries (ten)
Ice (two)
Milk (half a litre)
Equipment
Bowl, Sharp Knife, Chopping Board and Hand Blender
Method
- Get your banana, chop it up using a sharp knife but remember to put a chopping board underneath.
- Put the banana to one side.
- Leave the blueberries how they are.
- Now get your bowl and pour the banana and blueberries carefully into it.
- Add half a litre of milk and two ice cubes.
- Now get your hand blender and carefully put it in the bowl.
- Whisk it up till your lumps and bumps have vanished.
- Carefully pour your mixture into a cup.
- If you have any mini umbrellas put them in and if you want you can use a straw.

Emily Hockin
Year 5
Sprowston Junior School

GLOSSARY AND ABBREVIATIONS

Glossary

Cream: To make food into a smooth thick liquid.
Sift: To put flour, sugar, etc. through a sieve.
Simmer: To cook something liquid, or something that has liquid in it, at a temperature slightly below boiling.
Steam: The hot gas that is produced when water boils.
Score: To make a mark or a cut on a hard surface with a pointed tool.
Dice: To cut food into small squares.
Puree: To make fruit or vegetables into a thick smooth sauce.
Hulled: To take the stem and leaves from a fruit or vegetables
Knead: To press something with your hands and fingers repeatedly.
Strain: To become stretched or to experience pressure.
To seal: To close an entrance or container so that nothing can enter or leave it.
Season: To improve the flavor of savory food by adding salt, herbs or spices
Tender: (of meat or vegetables) easy to cut or chew.
Sear: To fry a piece of meat quickly at a high temperature, in order to prevent liquid and flavor escaping from it.
Reduced: To make something smaller in size, amount, degree.
Infuse: If you infuse a drink or it infuses, you leave substances such as tea leaves or herbs in hot water so that their flavor goes into the liquid.
Sauté: To cook food in oil or fat over heat, usually until it is brown.
Tepid: (of liquid) not very warm.

Abbreviations

- oz- Ounces
- g- Grams
- lb- Pounds
- ins- Inches
- ml- Millilitres
- cm- Centimetres
- F/C- Fahrenheit/centigrade

Many recipes use spoons as measurements- either a teaspoon (5ml), a dessertspoon (10ml) or a tablespoon (15ml). Unless the recipe says otherwise the measure is level

- Tbsp/Tblsp- Table spoon (15ml)
- Tsp- Tea spoon (5ml)
- Pkt- Packet

We didn't know the difference between a Sheriff and a Lord Mayor, so we looked it up and here it is!

Sheriff of Norwich

From 1403 until 1835 Norwich was able to elect one mayor and two sheriffs annually. This 432 year old privilege was abolished by the municipal Reform Act, which meant only one sheriff could be elected from 1835 onwards. In 1909 the 506 year old status of mayor was elevated to lord mayor by King Edward VII. Norwich is one of the only 15 UK towns and cities to appoint a sheriff. The appointment is made annually. Members of the majority political group on the Council make the decision as to who is to become sheriff. The role is honorary and apolitical.

Lord Mayor of Norwich

Norwich is one of the only cities to appoint a lord mayor. The appointment is made annually. Nominations can only be received from serving Norwich city councillors. Members of the majority political group on the council make the decision as to who is to become Lord Mayor. The role is primarily ceremonial and apolitical.

Each new lord mayor and sheriff take up their new positions in a special ceremony held on the council s annual general meeting in May each year.

TOP TIPS

- Any cooking involving more than a bowl and a wooden spoon it's best to have an **adult with you**, especially if you need to use a cooker or sharp knives
- Always wash your hands well before you start working with the ingredients, and wear an apron
- If you have long hair remember to tie it back
- Have all the ingredients and equipment ready before you start cooking
- Don't use any food that has expired (past it's sell by date)
- If you are using fruit or vegetables, wash them before
- Follow the instructions carefully
- Use oven gloves when using the oven
- Remember if you cook, you should wash up!

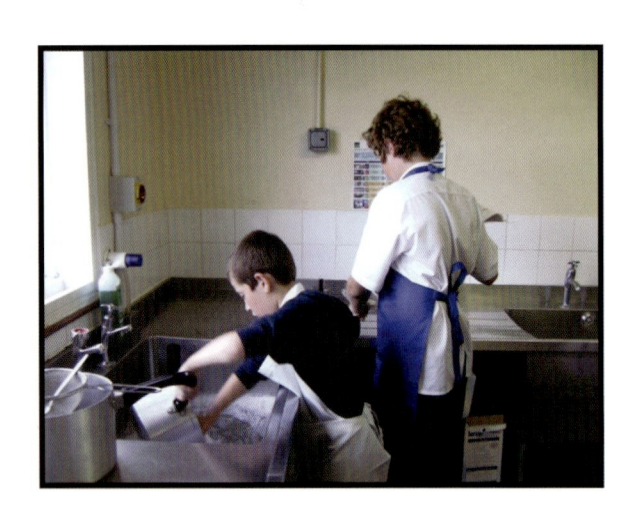

ESSENTIAL KITCHEN EQUIPMENT

- Bowls
- Knives, forks, spoons and kitchen scissors
- Baking paper/trays/cake tins
- Saucepans
- Whisk
- Chopping boards (different boards needed for different foods, eg. Don't cut onions and strawberries on the same board!)
- Grater
- Kitchen scales

OUR THANKS

In no particular order;

To Geoff Tucker, Sales Director at Norse, who believed in us and what we wanted to achieve, and Norse for their significant contribution to getting this book printed. www.ncsgrp.co.uk

To the following companies who also sponsored us so we could afford to get the book printed;
Hydrogen www.h2publicity.com
Bayer CropScience www.bayercropscience.co.uk
DBC Food Service www.dbcfoodservice
To the Chadacre Trust www.chadacre-trust.org.uk for a grant. Without these five contributors the book would never have been printed.

To Steve Butcher who provided us with the software to put the book together, and taught us how to use it. www.2mphotobooks.com

To the following who provided prizes for the children whose recipes we choose to go into the book;
Hugh Dennis, comedian and actor (the Dad in BBC TV programme 'Outnumbered') for his signed photograph,
Roys (Wroxham) Limited, the Theatre Royal, Hollywood and Odeon Cinemas, John Lewis, Norse and 2MPrint.
We had enough prizes for each child whose recipe is included. The 'Star Recipe' was 'Mediterranean Tartlets' sent in by the Cookery Club from Edward Worlledge Community Junior School. They won a digital camera. The two schools that sent the most recipes were Arden Grove Infant and Nursery School and Woodland View Junior School. These schools were given an additional prize.

To Alex Lynch, Change4Life Coordinator, NHS Norfolk who helped us with the page about Healthy Food and Healthy Eating.

To Lincoln Southgate, Solicitor from Norfolk County Council who gave us advice about copyright.

To Norse Catering for allowing Linda Bean (Mobile Cook Manager) and Ros Storey (Key Account Manager) to cook the adult recipes with help from Claire West, our school Cook in Charge and also to Elaine Breeze and Jenny Leslie who still managed to cook our lunches that morning when the recipe testing was being done.

To our parents and family members who had the fun of tasting the recipes, as well as Kinsale Junior school pupils who bought the cakes and biscuits (raising £50 for EAAA) to taste, and provided us with written comments. To Mrs West's Cookery Club who also tested and tasted some of the recipes.

To Galton Blackiston, Chef and The Earl of Iveagh, Trustee of the EAAA for writing a foreword.

To Simon Newbery, Managing Director of Orchard Toys for allowing Heather Yates, one of their designers to design our fabulous book cover. (You may notice it's similar to the design of our board game 'Norfolk's Fine Food'). www.orchardtoys.com

To Jess Down, Area Fundraising Manager, Norwich & North Norfolk, EAAA and Laura Shearing for their interest and support.

To all the adults who sent us a recipe, a photograph of themselves and took time to provide some text about themselves.

To all the Norfolk school children who sent us their recipes.

YOUR OWN RECIPE

NOTES